Coyote & Bobcat

Illustrated by Kathy Kifer and Dahna Solar

Ane Rovetta
Story consultant

Published by:
Garlic Press
605 Powers St.
Eugene, OR 97402

ISBN 0-931993-81-4
Order No. GP-081

www.garlicpress.com

Introducing the **Sign Language Literature Series**

    The **Sign Language Literature Series** presents
stories from different cultures. Many North American
native people tell coyote stories. In their stories,
coyote is usually a clever and resilient character with
a powerful imagination. His adventures cast him as
hero as often as a seeming fool.
    Coyote and Bobcat is adapted from a Navajo story.
It serves to explain how the coyote and the bobcat got
their shapes. The story is presented in simple
language, full illustration, and complemented with
illustrated signs.

Long ago | Bobcat | very

good | hunter. (hunt + animal)

Coyote | jealous.

A long time ago, Bobcat was a very good
hunter. Coyote was jealous.

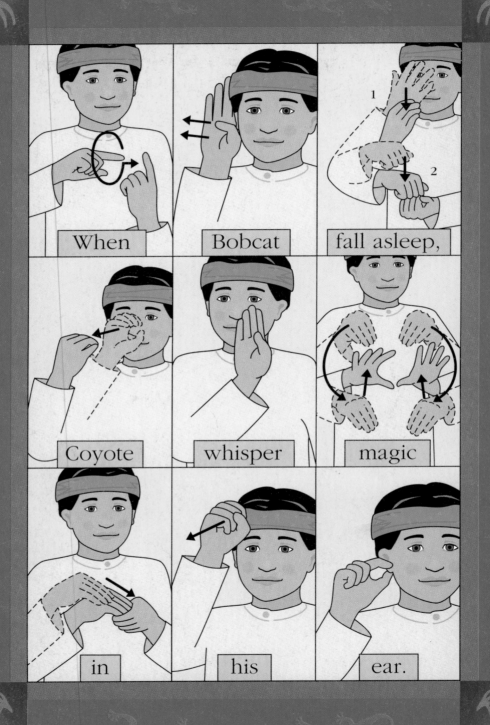

When   Bobcat   fall asleep,

Coyote   whisper   magic

in   his   ear.

When Bobcat fell asleep,
Coyote whispered magic in his ear.

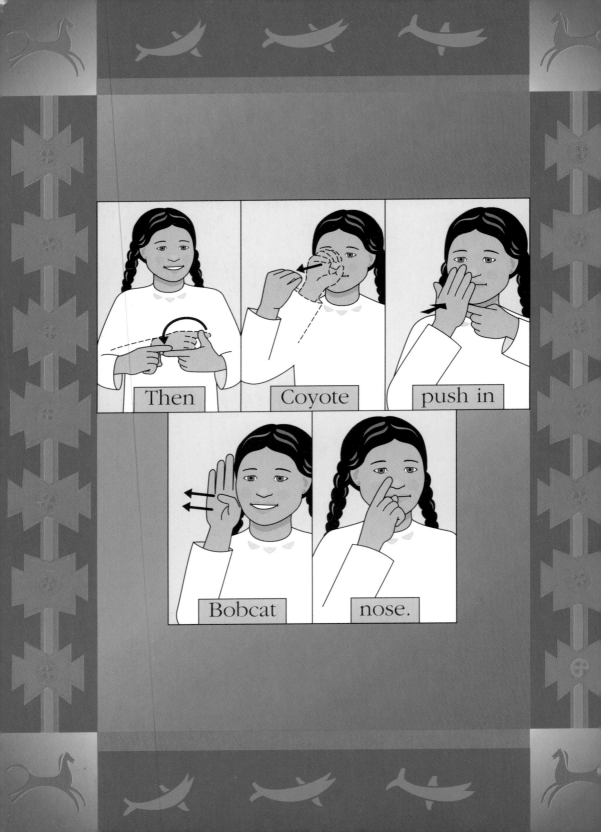

Then   Coyote   push in

Bobcat   nose.

Then Coyote pushed in
Bobcat's nose.

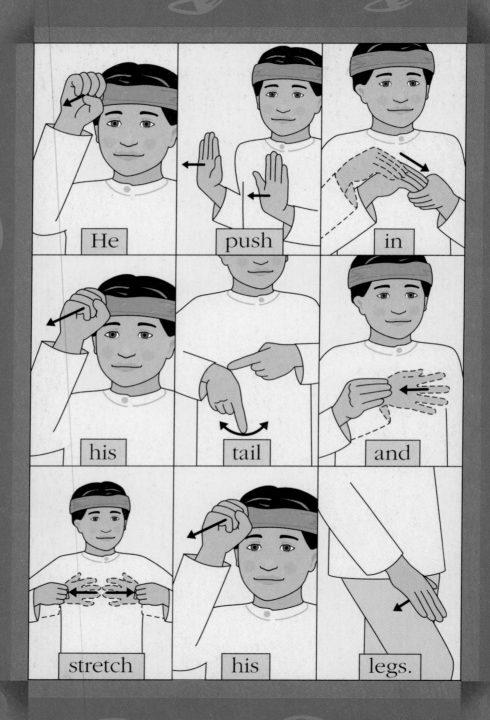

He pushed in his tail and
stretched his legs.

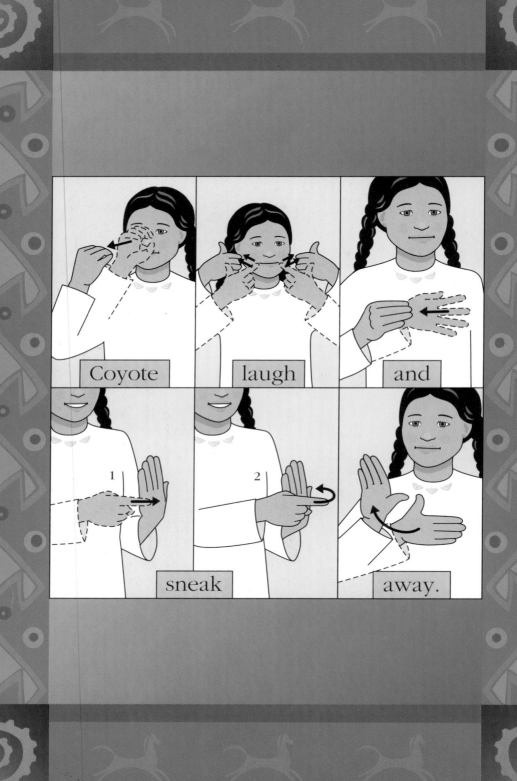

Coyote laugh and sneak away.

Coyote laughed and
snuck away.

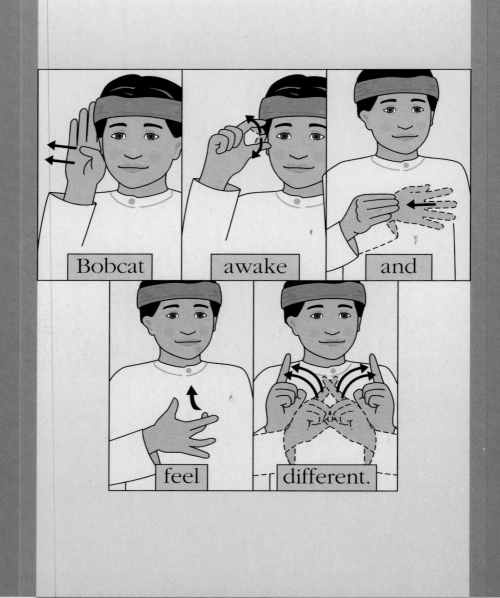

Bobcat awake and feel different.

Bobcat awoke and
felt different.

He see reflection

in lake and

understand why.

He saw his reflection in the lake
and understood why.

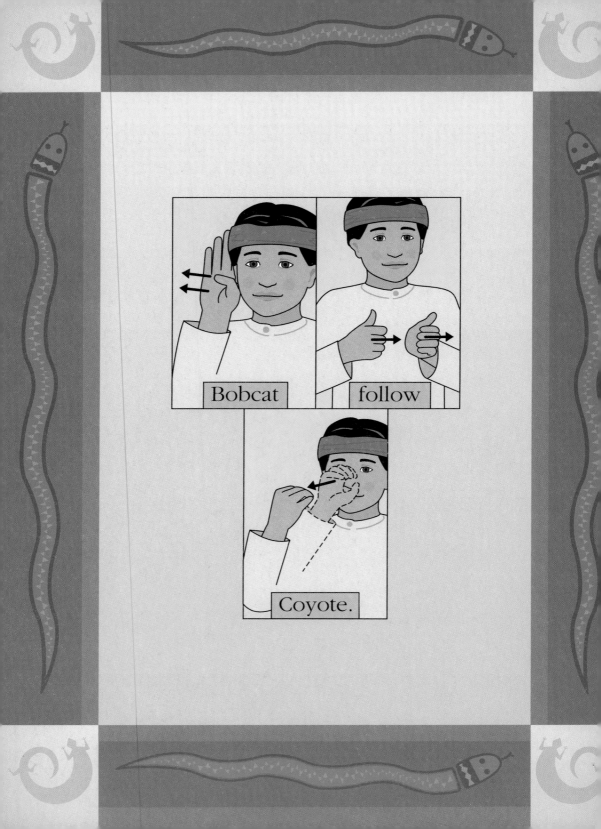

Bobcat

follow

Coyote.

Bobcat followed Coyote.

He soon found Coyote asleep.

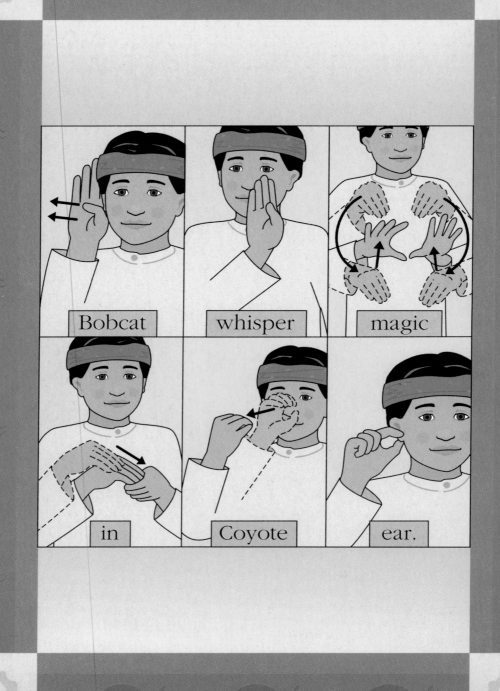

Bobcat whispered magic in Coyote's ear.

Bobcat pull Coyote nose to point. He pull his tail until stay down.

Bobcat pulled Coyote's nose to a point.
He pulled his tail until it stayed down.

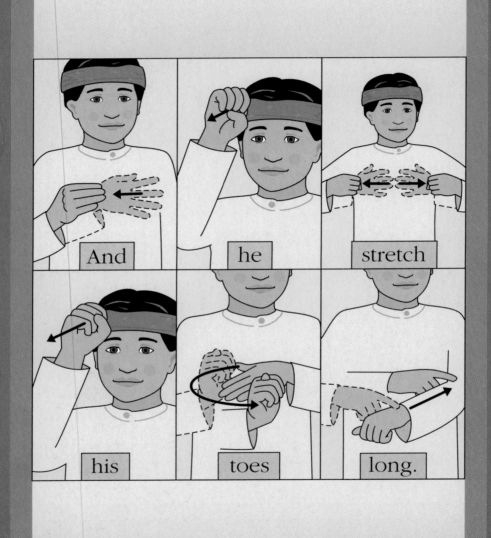

And he stretch his toes long.

And he stretched his toes long.

And that is

why Coyote and Bobcat

look so different from

each other.

And that is why Coyote and Bobcat
look so different from each other.

Also from Garlic Press

Finger Alphabet GP-046
Uses word games and activities to teach the finger alphabet.

Signing in School GP-047
Presents signs needed in a school setting.

Can I Help? Helping the Hearing Impaired in Emergency Situations
GP-057 Signs, sentences and information to help communicate with the hearing impaired.

Caring for Young Children: Signing for Day Care Providers and Sitters
GP-058 Signs for feelings, directions, activities and foods, bedtime, discipline and comfort-giving.

An Alphabet of Animal Signs
GP-065 Animal illustrations and associated signs for each letter of the alphabet.

Mother Goose in Sign
GP-066 Fully illustrated nursery rhymes.

Number and Letter Games
GP-072 Presents a variety of games involving the finger alphabet and sign numbers.

Expanded Songs in Sign
GP-005 Eleven songs in Signed English. The easy-to-follow illustrations enable you to sign along.

Foods GP-087
A colorful collection of photos with signs for 43 common foods.

Fruits & Vegetables GP-088
Thirty-nine beautiful photos with signs.

Pets, Animals & Creatures
GP-089 Seventy-seven photos with signs of pets, animals & creatures familiar to signers of all ages.

Signing at Church
GP-098 For adults and young adults. Helpful phrases, the Lord's Prayer and *John 3:16.*

Signing at Sunday School
GP-099 Phrases, songs, Bible verses and the story of Jesus clearly illustrated.

Family and Community
GP-073 Signs for relationships and family and community members in their job roles.

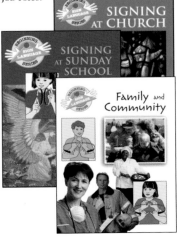

Coyote & Bobcat
GP-081 A Navajo story serving to tell how Coyote and Bobcat got their shapes.

Raven & Water Monster
GP-082 This Haida story tells how Raven gained his beautiful black color and how he brought water to the earth.

Fountain of Youth
GP-086 This Korean folk tale about neighbors shows the rewards of kindness and the folly of greed.

Ananse the Spider: Why Spiders Stay on the Ceiling
GP-085 A West African folk tale about the boastful spider Ananse and why he now hides in dark corners.

www.garlicpress.com